n

STICKMEN'S GUIDE TO GIGANTIC MACHINES

Thanks to the creative team:

Senior Editor: Alice Peebles

Designer: Lauren Woods and collaborate agency

Original edition copyright 2015 by Hungry Tomato Ltd.

Hungry Tomato™
A division of Lerner Publishing Group, Inc.
241 First Avenue North
Minneapolis, MN 55401 USA

For reading levels and more information, look up this title at www.lernerbooks.com.

Main body text set in Century Gothic.

Typeface provided by Monotype Typography.

Library of Congress Cataloging-in-Publication Data

Farndon, John, author.
    Stickmen's Guide to gigantic machines / by John Farndon ; illustrated by John Paul de Quay.
        pages cm. — (Stickmen's guides to how everything works)
    Audience: Ages 8-12.
    Audience: Grades 4 to 6.
    Summary: "Whimsical stick figure guides take readers on a tour of various massive machines and how they work in this playful yet extremely informative guide to high-tech machines."— Provided by publisher.
    Includes index.
    ISBN 978-1-4677-9361-2 (lb : alk. paper) — ISBN 978-1-4677-9595-1 (pb : alk. paper) — ISBN 978-1-4677-9596-8 (eb pdf)
    1. Machinery—Juvenile literature. 2. Technology—Juvenile literature. I. de Quay, John Paul, illustrator. II. Title. III. Title: Guide to gigantic machines.
TJ147.O886 2016
621—dc23   2015032762

Manufactured in the United States of America
1 – VP – 12/31/15

STICKMEN'S GUIDE TO GIGANTIC MACHINES

by John Farndon
Illustrated by John Paul de Quay

HUNGRY TOMATO.

Germany's bucket
wheel excavator
is as long as two
football fields.

Contents

Gigantic Machines

You are completely surrounded by machines. Scissors, computers, central heating systems, screwdrivers, door handles, bicycles, and countless other things are all machines. Most of these are human-sized. But the machines in this book are truly monstrous. They're all made by humans, of course, but they are so big they seem like the machines of giants.

The Factory Machine

The biggest machines in the world are actually factories. Some factories need a lot of help from workers to make things. But in many of the largest car factories, more and more of the work is done by robots. Modern car factories, such as BMW's in Munich *(right)*, are like scenes from *Transformers*, with robot arms whirling relentlessly as they put together car after car.

The World's Smallest Machines

The machines in this book are awesomely big. But there are now machines that are just as awesomely tiny. They are called nanomachines and are so small you can see them only under the most powerful electron microscopes. One team at Rice University in Texas made a car no bigger than a molecule. But perhaps the most exciting are the nanorobot doctors being developed. They can be injected into your bloodstream to investigate and repair damage or even deliver drugs to exactly the right place inside the body.

Mystery Stone Movers

All over the world, prehistoric people left behind giant stones called megaliths. The biggest underpin an ancient temple at Baalbek in Lebanon. They weigh up to 1,600 tons each, and no one knows how they were moved from the quarry 0.5 mile (800 m) away. French archaeologist Jean-Pierre Adam thinks it was with machines that we now know nothing about, involving rollers, winding cables, and pulleys.

Big Pit

Some of the biggest machines in this book are diggers, designed to excavate pits like the enormous Bingham Canyon copper mine near Salt Lake City in Utah. Machines dig out nearly half a million tons of rock here every day and have made a hole 2.75 miles (4.4 km) across and 0.75 mile (1.2 km) deep. If this were a basketball stadium, it would have room for every single person in New York City and a few more.

The Farthest Machines

No machines are farther away than Voyagers 1 and 2. These space probes, launched in 1977, have been heading out into space ever since. Voyager 1 is 12 billion miles away and Voyager 2 is 10 billion miles away—and they are getting hundreds of miles farther away every second. Voyager 1 zoomed entirely out of the solar system in 2012.

History of Gigantic Machines

The story of enormous machines goes further back in time than you might imagine. Many of the biggest machines have been built since the Industrial Revolution two centuries or so ago. But some extraordinary machines existed in the ancient world, too, in ancient Egypt, Greece, Rome, and China.

1st century CE
The Roman Barbegal mills in France used a staircase of 16 giant waterwheels to grind huge quantities of wheat (4.5 tons a day) into flour. A big round for the Romans!

340 BCE
Ancient Greek engineer Polydus of Thessaly invented Helepolis, the biggest siege machine ever: a 130-ft (40-m) armor-plated tower on wheels designed to attack city walls. It got stuck in the mud.

2000 BCE	1300 BCE	600 BCE	200 BCE

3000 BCE
The ancient Egyptians developed the ramp to build their gigantic stone pyramids. The work was inclined to be hard.

214 BCE
Scientist and inventor Archimedes of Syracuse in Sicily created a giant crane with an iron claw. It ripped attacking Roman ships from the water. Things picked up for the Syracusans.

Around 1187 CE

Kurdish military engineer Mardi ibn Ali al-Tarsusi wrote about giant counterweight trebuchets—catapult machines that could sling missiles as big as cars at the enemy. They had it coming.

1839

American William Otis (cousin of elevator inventor Elisha Otis) invented the steam shovel, the grandaddy of all mechanical excavators. It got him into a big hole.

1907

The Titan Crane was erected in Clydebank, UK, to help build ships such as the *Queen Elizabeth*. At the time it was the world's largest cantilever or "hammerhead" crane and the first electric crane. It could lift 160 tons (equivalent to 26 African elephants).

50 CE   650   1200   2000

1780

Lift locks capable of lifting entire barges from one canal level to another were invented. The oldest preserved example is the Anderton Boat Lift in Cheshire, UK, dating from 1875. The world's biggest boat lift, the one at the Three Gorges Dam in China, can raise entire cargo ships!

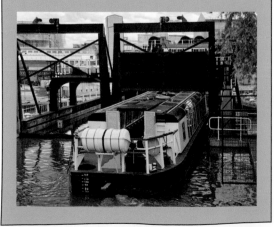

1913

Henry Ford created the first car assembly line to make Model T Ford cars in large numbers—and the first traffic jams.

1825

British engineer Marc Isambard Brunel invented the tunnel boring machine to create a tunnel under the River Thames. Only the mud got bored.

Dump Trucks

Mining companies need huge quantities of rocks moved fast—and the best way to do this is with giant dump trucks, sometimes called haul trucks. These big-as-a-house mine monsters never have to go on the road, so there is no limit to size: the bigger the better. All that matters is moving loads of rubble, fast. But mines are very tough, so these trucks have to be super-tough too.

Brute force

The powerhouse of a haul truck has to be unstoppable. That's why trucks like the BelAZ 75710 have two engines, not one, and both are 16-cylinder diesels. The engines are simply generators that produce the electricity to drive hugely powerful electric motors on four of the wheels, turning them directly.

The cab

The driver's cab is so small compared to the truck that you can barely see it. To reach it, the driver has to climb a ladder. The driver, of course, has power-assisted steering to turn those mighty wheels!

Turning tight

The truck has to make turns in tight places, so the front wheels can swivel a long way. That means a haul truck like the BelAZ 75710 can turn completely around in its own length.

The tipper

To empty the load, the front end of the hopper is powered up by massive hydraulic rams. When raised, the top of the hopper is higher than a five-story building!

Big Digger

Haul trucks often get their loads direct from another huge machine, a mechanical digger. This is like a giant shovel that digs out the ground with a bucket moved by a hinged arm. The arm gets its power from hydraulic (fluid-filled) pistons. The digging arm and cabin are on a swiveling turntable so it can be easily maneuvered.

High and Mighty

The biggest dump truck in the world is the BelAZ 75710 made in Belarus. It can move more than 450 tons of rubble in a single load. That's the weight of 250 or so cars, or 40 African elephants! To shift all that weight, it has an engine with a torque (turning force) of 13,738 lb-ft—about 24 times that of a 2014 Formula One racing car!

How Much?

If you wanted to buy a BelAZ 75710, it would cost you a cool $6,000,000…

The hopper

The load is carried in the truck's hopper, which is made from massively thick steel to take the weight and the constant battering of rubble. The hopper is filled by mechanical diggers or an overhead conveyor. But it needs to be unloaded instantly. That's why the hopper is designed to tip up, so the load can slide straight out.

Big wheels

Monster dump trucks run on what may be the world's biggest wheels. They're typically taller than an African elephant—about the height of two tall adult humans put together. And there are usually six or eight of them, each with absolutely massive rubber tires. Those tires are supremely tough and chunky—you don't want a flat with one of these!

Construction Cranes

Right now, scores of buildings more than 1,000 ft (300 m) tall are going up in cities all over the world. To build them, they need cranes that are just as tall—the tallest ever built. And these cranes don't just need to be tall. They have to lift very heavy weights and maneuver them to exactly where they are needed. This high up, even a small error could be disastrous.

Operator's cab

A crane operator's job is a tough one. You really need a head for heights. You have to be in shape, too. Every morning you climb ladders all the way up to the cab and, usually, drop in through the roof. Once inside, you'll be there all day—until you climb all the way back down again.

Slew control swivels the jib one way or the other

A trolley moves the hoist unit in and out along the arm to get the load exactly where it's needed.

The hook that lifts the load is attached to the hoist unit.

The hoist unit

Hoist control lever starts the hoist winding up or down

Computer screen shows the weight of the load, the climb speed, wind speed, and much more

Electronic systems ensure the load and hoist speed are perfectly matched

Video systems give the operator a close-up view of the hook and load

Windows are made of laminated safety glass

The Tallest Ever

The world's tallest cranes are not at their full height yet. These are the Liebherr cranes being used to build what will be the world's tallest building: the Kingdom Tower *(left)* in Jeddah, Saudi Arabia. The biggest, used in constructing the central tower, is a climbing crane, which means it will get taller as the building rises, using it as support. The last section of crane, for lifting the top of the building into place, will be over 3,280 ft (1,000 m) up! Yet the crane will still be only 8 ft (2.4 m) wide.

The jib is the long arm that carries the load.

The load is hoisted by a powerful electric motor or winch that winds a strong metal cable in or out.

Balancing act

Lifting a load on a crane is a careful balancing act. There has to be a counterweight of concrete blocks on the end of the machinery arm, opposite the jib, to balance out the load. The crane's motors also add to the counterweight.

The Cab

Putting Up a Climbing Crane

• The crew start by erecting a 40-ft (12-m) section of mast with the aid of a mobile crane.

• Then they put the jib, machinery arm, and slewing gear on top.

• A climbing frame is inserted between the slewing gear and the top of the mast.

• The climbing frame lifts the slewing gear on hydraulic rams.

• A new 20-ft (6-m) section is lifted by the crane itself and slotted into the gap opened by the climbing frame.

• Every time they want the crane to go higher, they use the climbing frame to open a new gap and insert an extra 20 ft (6 m) of mast.

The machinery arm is the shorter arm, opposite the jib, that carries the motor and the counterweights.

The slewing unit or turntable is a large ring gear and motor at the top of the tower that allows the jib to swivel.

Hydraulic climbing frame

The crane's mast is a lattice structure made of triangular diagonal bars.

At its base, the crane is bolted into concrete with giant anchor bolts, to keep it from toppling over.

Material scooped up by the bucket wheel drops through a chute onto a conveyor.

Each bucket can hold 3,400 dry gallons (15 m³) of earth—that's about 184 bathtubs full.

Cutting boom hoist rope

At the inner end of the cutting boom, material falls onto another conveyor to be carried out along the discharge boom.

Superstructure holds the boom hoist mechanism

Hoist mechanism for raising or lowering the cutting boom, taking about five minutes

The bucket wheel is a giant wheel with up to 20 buckets to scoop earth as the wheel rotates.

The bucket wheel is mounted on the front end of an arm called the cutting boom.

The conveyor carries material back along the cutting boom.

Using a BWE such as the Bagger 293, five workers can do the same job as 40,000 miners.

The machine sits on electric-powered crawlers (wheels wrapped with a flexible track), which allow its massive weight to move across soft ground.

Bucket Wheel Excavators

Gigantic bucket wheel excavators (BWEs) are the world's most monstrous vehicles. With their whirling bucket wheels they can chew through the ground at a furious rate. The biggest can shift hundreds of thousands of tons of ground material, carving a deep gouge in the earth.

Big Bagger

The biggest BWE, and the biggest vehicle ever, is the Bagger 293 *(left)*, which mines brown coal near Hambach in Germany. It's 738 ft (225 m) long and 315 ft (96 m) tall—about as wide and a bit taller than the Capitol building in Washington, DC. It also weighs a crushing 14,200 tons! And it has wheels—or, rather, crawlers.

Turntable allows the mechanism to swivel or "slew" around, in about half an hour

Counterweight boom balances the weight of the cutting wheel

Mobile conveyors stand ready to collect the material coming off the end of the discharge boom and dump it into trucks for disposal

The Bagger 293 can race along at over 30 ft (9 m) per minute, or about 0.3 mph (0.5 km/h).

The coal dug by the Bagger 293 in one day would fill 2,400 coal wagons.

The large area of the crawlers spreads the weight so wide that a BWE can move over grass without damaging it.

Tunneling Machines

If you want to dig a really big tunnel, you need a boring machine—a tunnel-boring machine, or TBM. These are gigantic drills that bore through the ground, leaving a complete tunnel behind them. Without them, city subway systems, water mains, and road and other tunnels could not be built.

A typical TBM is 450 ft (137 m) long (as long as two giant Airbus A380 airliners) and 25 ft (7.6 m) in diameter.

A TBM weighs about 1,000 tons.

An inbuilt laser guidance system helps the tunneling team keep the machine on course.

Ground and crushed rock is fed back through the shield and onto a continuously running conveyor belt.

As the cutterhead moves forward, precast segments of concrete wall are lifted into place with a lifting device inside the shield.

The concrete segments are built up into a ring by a device called an erector and pushed out at the back of the shield to form a new section of tunnel wall.

The conveyor belt carries the loose rock away from the back of the shield and out of the tunnel.

The space between the rock and the concrete ring is filled and sealed with cement.

The TBM needs only a small team, and the operator controlling the cutterhead sits a ways behind in a control booth, monitoring progress on screens fed by cameras at the head. →

A

B

Workers' break room

The electric and hydraulic power systems are behind the cutter.

Pressure sensors continually monitor the turning power of the cutterhead, and adjustments are made automatically.

The front of the TBM is a cylinder called a shield, because it shields the tunnelers as they dig.

The cutterhead is driven around by powerful electric motors and grinds away the rock.

Powerful hydraulic rams press the cutterhead up against the rock face.

The front of the shield is a giant disc facing into the new rock. It's called the cutterhead and is fitted with incredibly tough steel-cutting edges and scrapers.

B

Big Bertha Gets Stuck

North America's biggest borer is Big Bertha, named after the USA's first female mayor, Bertha Knight Landes, who was mayor of Seattle in the 1920s. Big Bertha weighs 7,000 tons and has a cutterhead 57.5 ft (17.5 m) in diameter. In 2013, it began drilling a massive double-decker highway tunnel in Seattle, cutting through 30 ft (9 m) of solid rock every day. But after 1,000 ft (300 m), it ground to a halt after grit got into its bearings. Engineers took over a year to work out how to replace the bearings!

Combine Harvesters

When harvest time comes each year, wheat fields around the world begin to throb with the sound of giant machines called combine harvesters. Their task is to cut down the ripe wheat and gather the grain to make the flour we need for our bread. The world's biggest combine harvester, the Lexion 780, can gather over 700 tons of grain in a day—enough to make nearly a million loaves!

6 The stalks move back on conveyors called straw walkers, which have a walking motion to shake off any remaining grain into the tank.

4 The cut stalks are drawn by an auger (corkscrew) towards the center and whisked up a conveyor belt called an elevator into the harvester's processing mechanism.

8 The tailings are chopped up and carried out the back, to drop on the field as straw.

7 To winnow the grain, air is blasted through it to blow off the chaff, which is then sieved off and blown back onto the field.

5 Rotors thresh the crop, beating the stalks to separate the grain, which drops into a collecting tank.

3 As the pick-up reel pushes them back, the stalks are snipped off just above the ground by the cutter bar.

All-in-One Harvesters

Combine harvesters get their name from combining all the tasks needed to gather wheat. As they drive through a field of ripe wheat or any other cereal crop, they cut the stalks, separate the grain, and clean and collect it automatically, using rotating blades, wheels, sieves, and conveyors. They combine the three main tasks in harvesting:

- Reaping—cutting and gathering the stalks

- Threshing—shaking or beating the stalks to loosen the grain from the "tailings," the stalks that become straw

- Winnowing—getting rid of the scaly unwanted "chaff" that holds the grain

Tiring Work

Hefty farm machines have to cross soft earth and mud in all kinds of terrain and weather. So they have some of the biggest, chunkiest tires in the world. The biggest tractor tires are almost 9 ft (2.7 m) tall.

9 When the grain tank is full, the grain is carried up from the tank by an elevator and shoots out of a side pipe (sometimes called the unloader) into a waiting trailer.

2 The slowly rotating pick-up reel has teeth and bars called bats that push the stalks toward the cutter.

1 The header gathers the stalks in at the front with a pair of sharp pincers called crop dividers.

Semisubmersible Rigs

Some of the best sources of oil and natural gas lie below the seabed. To get at them, oil rig workers have to set up huge drilling platforms out at sea. But what if the water is too deep to rest the supports for the platform on the seabed? Then what's needed is a semisubmersible rig, which rests on pontoons (tanks) that float just under the surface of the sea.

Mud is pumped down inside the drill "string"—its entire length.

The mud travels back up the casing of the bore, taking rock cuttings with it.

A nozzle sprays mud on the drill bit, cleaning the bit in the process.

String Time

The drill can reach 20,000 ft (6,096 m) into the seabed. Even under the sea, it could overheat when drilling into the solid rock of the seabed. So it is kept lubricated, cooled, and clean by continuously pumping in a special fluid called drilling mud. The mud also brings the cuttings (drilled rock fragments) up to the surface.

Tough Bits

The head of the drill, or drill bit, turns continuously and cuts slowly into the rock. Its cutting edges are toughened with different materials according to the rock type. Such materials include steel, tungsten-carbide, PDC (synthetic diamond), or even real diamond.

Gusher!

Once the hole has been drilled, the oil has to be extracted. So the rig workers reinforce the newly drilled hole with a casing of concrete. Next, they make little holes in the casing near the bottom to let oil in, and top the well with a "Christmas tree" of control valves. Finally, they send down acid or pressurized sand to break through the last layer of rock. The oil then gushes up through the pipe under its own pressure.

A helipad makes it easy to get to and from the platform by helicopter.

The high drill tower allows pieces to be added to the drill string as it goes deeper.

A swivel mechanism enables the drill string to rotate.

The drill crew works, eats, and sleeps aboard the platform.

The platform sits on tall legs up to 10,000 ft (3,000 m) above the seabed. The legs raise it out of reach of the waves, keeping it stable.

Lifeboats are essential in case of emergency.

The platform legs sit on pontoons filled with ballast (weights) so they float deep below the water, unaffected by waves.

The pontoons are anchored in place to the sea floor by cables.

Mud supply for cooling and lubricating the drill

Rig Building

Semisubmersibles are built almost entirely on shore, in shipyards. They are then launched into the water and dragged by powerful tugs to the place where they will be used. This can be many thousands of miles away.

To reach all the way down to the seabed, the drill is built up piece by piece to make a long "string."

Casing

Drill collar

Mud pump

The drill head bores through the seabed rock to reach the oil

Control Room

When moving a spacecraft as tall as a skyscraper, the crew have to keep the platform level. The top of the spacecraft cannot be out of vertical by even a fraction. In the control room, they check the level constantly with laser and electronic technology and make adjustments with the JEL (Jacking, Equalization, and Leveling) system.

There is a driver's cab at each corner: two for when the crawler is going backward and two for when it's moving forward.

The four generators provide electric power for the 16 traction motors that drive the wheels.

Originally, the crawlers could carry a staggering 7,000-ton load, but they have been upgraded to take over 9,000 tons.

The crawler is operated by a team of 30 engineers, technicians, and drivers.

The crawler's flat top allows it to slide under the launch platform to pick up the entire platform and tower, along with its spacecraft load.

Two giant diesel engines, each generating 2,750 horsepower, drive four electricity generators, one for each track unit.

Crawler Vehicles

Hans and Franz are the crawler vehicles used at the Kennedy Space Center in the USA. Their task is to carry spacecraft from the buildings where they are assembled to the launchpads, ready to be blasted into space. They are the world's biggest self-propelled vehicles. Bucket wheel excavators may be bigger, but only Hans and Franz can move under their own power.

What Do They Carry?

- The crawlers were originally built to move the giant Saturn V rockets that carried the Apollo moon missions. That meant they were carrying a rocket that was 363 ft (110 m) tall, as well as its 398-ft (121-m) launch tower.

- After the Apollo and Skylab missions finished in 1979, the crawlers were reused for over 30 years to carry the shuttles and their boosters into place for launch.

- Revamped, one crawler will now take commercial rockets to the launchpad, while the other will carry the 320-ft (97.5-m) Space Launch System designed to launch missions to Mars.

The crawlers are 131 ft (40 m) long and 113 ft (34 m) wide.

The height of the crawler can be altered from 20 ft (6 m) to 26 ft (8 m).

The track units can swivel independently to steer the crawler.

The crawler runs on four track units, each with two tracks, and each powered by four electric motors.

Jacking cylinders can raise each side independently by up to 6 ft (1.8 m) to keep the platform completely level.

The crawlers can reach a speed of 1 mph (1.6 km/h) loaded and 2 mph (3.2 km/h) unloaded.

The crawler weighs 2,750 tons without a load.

Each track is made from 57 steel shoes.

The wheels run around inside their own moving track, which spreads the load.

Each shoe is 7 ft (2.1 m) long and 1.5 ft (0.45 m) wide, and weighs a ton.

Large Hadron Collider

The best way to find out what atoms are made of is to smash them together so they break apart. To do this, scientists build giant machines called particle accelerators in deep tunnels. Here, powerful magnets accelerate particles to high speeds and hurl them together. The Large Hadron Collider (LHC) is the biggest.

Electromagnet coil

Inner detectors

Heat detectors

Muon detectors

The Detectors

Around the ring there are six detectors that scientists use to make observations and perform experiments. They are a bit like digital cameras. Although the particles they study are tiny, the detectors can be as much as three stories high and weigh more than 5,000 tons. The biggest is ATLAS. It is so big and complicated it had to be taken underground in pieces and took five years to assemble. Its task is to detect collisions between protons.

Giant Research Project

The LHC is located deep underground on the border between Switzerland and France. It is run by CERN, the European Organization for Nuclear Research.

The Higgs Boson

The LHC has become famous for its hunt for a special particle called the Higgs Boson. Scientists think this mysterious particle may explain why things have mass—that is, why some things are light and others heavy. In 2013, they confirmed that they had seen it in the LHC, but no one knows quite what that means yet.

The particles race around in a very narrow pipe within the service tunnel, held on course by 9,600 additional magnets.

The pipe is an extreme vacuum inside and is heavily insulated to keep particles from escaping.

Incredibly powerful electromagnets accelerate the particles again and again as they hurtle around the tunnel until they reach 99.9 percent of the speed of light.

Scientists and engineers get down to the machinery by several elevators.

The tunnels are over 300 ft (90 m) below ground to protect the LHR from any radiation from space.

The LHC uses 10,800 tons of liquid nitrogen and helium to cool the magnets down to -456.25°F (-271.25°C). This makes them work better.

The tunnel is 16.8 miles (27 km) around.

ATLAS is the biggest detector.

The detector records particle collisions like a giant electronic camera.

25

The top of the first hill is the highest point of the ride. So it has maximum potential energy. From this point, it can only go downhill... or can it?

Wheels All Around

A roller coaster needs special wheels to hold it to the track as it roars from side to side and even goes upside down. Ordinary train wheels can run only on top of the track. But roller-coaster wheels must run on top, along the side, and underneath, too.

When you zoom down the slopes, you go into free fall and float off the seat, apparently weightless.

As the cars hurtle faster and faster down the first slope, they gain kinetic energy— the energy of motion.

After whizzing down the first hill, the cars have huge momentum. This means they are so loaded with kinetic energy that they can zoom right up again— either high up another hill or around in a loop.

= acceleration

= centrifugal force

= gravity

Loop the Loop

As they loop, cars are held onto the track by the "apparent force" created by the tug-of-war between gravity and the changing direction of their own acceleration. Loops on roller coasters have to be teardrop-shaped, not round, to keep the forces in balance.

Roller Coasters

Roller coasters might look like very crazy trains. But these super-scary rides need no engine or power. They are driven by gravity and momentum alone. They only need power to launch them from the top of the first hill. After that, they just go and go...

Liftoff

On older roller coasters, the ride starts with a slow haul up the first, tallest hill (called the lift hill) by a chain that hooks into the base of the cars. The highter the train climbs, the further it has to fall and the more potential energy it gains—the energy of gravity.

Whoosh!

Instead of the slow crawl up the lift hill, modern roller coasters start with a power launch that blasts you straight to high speeds, using electromagnets, hydraulics, or compressed air. Within a few seconds of the start you may be traveling at 100 mph (160 km/h)!

As they race up the second loop, the cars gain new potential energy. It's not as much as at the start, but it's enough to give them a new burst of speed.

Shooting down the big loop, they gain enough kinetic energy to roar up the second loop. They've lost a bit of energy, though, so the second loop has to be smaller.

Climbing to the top of the second loop gives another boost in potential energy—enough to make the cars accelerate again.

The acceleration is just enough to give the cars the kinetic energy to climb the final slope, even though friction and air resistance begin to slow them down.

The cars are brought to a halt at the end by magnetic brakes.

Older roller coasters have wooden tracks, but most modern tracks are tubes of steel that can be twisted into all kinds of shapes.

Safety is vital on roller coasters, so riders are strapped or barred in securely before the ride.

Abrams Tank

Tanks are the most intimidating of all war machines, designed to blast their way across battlefields. They seem unstoppable with their huge weight, heavy armor, and enormous firepower. They can be stopped, but it is not easy, which is why the 68-ton M1 Abrams tank is one of the US Army's key battlefield weapons.

To load the main gun, missiles can be taken manually from the missile store, or it can load automatically.

The loader is helped to aim the gun by thermal sight goggles that reveal hot objects, such as a hot engine, even in pitch darkness.

Optical periscope

Commander's machine gun

Gun loader's hatch

The tank is powered by a mighty 1500-hp turbine.

To protect the crew in case of a hit, the fuel and ammunition are stored in armored compartments designed with blow-off panels that blow out, away from the crew.

Tracks bear the tank's huge weight by spreading the load and allow it to ride relentlessly over all kinds of terrain. The engine drives the wheels, which roll along the inside of the track, so that the track rolls forward.

Hiding

Two smoke grenade launchers on the turret can send up a cloud of smoke to hide the tank even from thermal imaging systems.

Countermeasures

Some Abrams tanks have a missile countermeasure device to interfere electronically with the guidance systems of enemy missiles.

The Driver

The tank driver slides in to lie back in the cramped space at the front of the tank, called the driver's station. There is no direct view out. Instead, he or she sees where to go through periscope views displayed on three screens.

Dials left to right: engine rev counter, speedometer, fuel gauge

Mission check

Damage warning lights

Left-hand track control

Right-hand track control

Engine power control

The gun turret swivels to aim the main gun in different directions

Driver's hatch

The main weapon is a 32.04-ft (9.7-m) M256A1 gun designed to destroy tanks, armored vehicles and low-flying aircraft

Fire brigade

The tank has its own instant fire extinguishers, in case the interior ever catches fire.

The Abrams tank's armor plating is not just thick steel—it is a multilayered shield of steel, ceramic, plastic, and Kevlar that offers much greater protection by absorbing some of the shock.

The front of the turret and hull get extra protection from a coating of very dense depleted uranium, which has the effect of a 2-ft (0.6-m) wall of steel.

To make it harder to spot, the tank is painted a flat green in wooded and grassy areas and tan in the desert.

Strange Inventions

Intriguing giant machine designs date from the earliest times...

Magic Doors

If you thought automatic doors were pretty modern, think again. Nearly 2,000 years ago, a mechanical genius called Hero, who lived in Alexandria in Egypt, invented a mechanism for opening the gigantic doors of Greek temples as if by magic. When the priests lit a fire on the altar, the hot air was used to move water, which then triggered an ingenious mechanism to move counterweights that swung the great doors open—and even blew hot air to create a blast on giant trumpets. No wonder visitors were awed.

Cosmic Clock

Robots may seem like recent creations, but inventors have been designing automata (machines that work by themselves) for thousands of years. One of the biggest was the Cosmic Engine of Chinese minister Su Sung. This was actually one of the first clocks. It was 30 ft (9 m) high and worked via rotating wheels and water pressure (or liquid mercury). At certain times of day, full-sized mechanical men and women at the top would ring bells and bash gongs. It ran for 30 years between 1092 and 1126 CE.

Giant Wood Ant

It looks like a terrifying, six-legged giant insect. In fact, the "walking harvester" by Plustech/Timberjack was the prototype for a real machine designed to help lumberjacks cut and gather trees in tricky terrain. The legs are moved in an ant-like way by computer, according to the driver's instructions. It has an antenna-like arm at the front for chopping down trees and picking them up.

Fountain Machine

King Louis XIV of France wanted the world's biggest fountains to shoot water into the air at his palace at Versailles. So he commissioned the Marly Machine, finished in 1684. This huge pumping machine, with its 250 pumps, used an array of giant paddles to force water 500 ft (152 m) up from the River Seine to the palace gardens. It pumped as much water every day as was consumed by the entire population of Paris.

The World's Biggest Spider

In 2008, French company La Machine presented their giant mechanical spider—just for fun—at a parade in Liverpool, UK, as part of the city's celebrations as European capital of culture. The towering arachnid, nicknamed "La Princesse," is 50 ft (15 m) tall and weighs 37 tons. It walks on eight legs with 50 hydraulically moved joints, and needs 12 people to operate it.

Glossary

Cutterhead

The cutting face of a tunnel-boring machine

Electromagnets

Powerful magnets activated by an electric current

Hadron

Any particle, such as protons and neutrons, made with a combination of quarks, the most basic particles of all

Haul truck

A giant dump truck used in mines and quarries

Hopper

An open container for loose bulk material that can be easily tipped or poured out

Hydraulic

Power system based on pushing fluids through tubes with pistons

Jib

The long arm that carries a crane's load

Kinetic energy

The energy something has because it is moving

Potential energy

The energy something has because of its position, typically its height above the ground

Reaping

Cutting and gathering the stalks when harvesting cereals

Slewing unit

The turntable at the top of the crane tower that allows the jib to swivel

Submersible

A craft or machine designed to work underwater

Threshing

Shaking or beating the stalks to loosen the grain when harvesting cereals

Torque

The turning force of an engine

Tower crane

A crane on a tall tower

Winnowing

Getting rid of scaly, unwanted chaff, which holds the grain, when harvesting cereals

INDEX

The Author

John Farndon is Royal Literary Fellow at Anglia Ruskin University in Cambridge, UK. He has written numerous books for adults and children on science, technology, and nature, and been shortlisted four times for the Royal Society's Young People's Book Prize. He has recently created science stories for children for the Moscow Polytech science festival.

The Illustrator

John Paul de Quay has a BSc in Biology from the University of Sussex, UK, and a graduate certificate in animation from the University of the West of England. He devotes his spare time to growing chilli peppers, perfecting his plan for a sustainable future, and caring for a small plastic dinosaur. He has three pet squid that live in the bath, which makes drawing in ink quite economical…

Picture Credits (abbreviations: t = top; b = bottom; c = center; l = left; r = right)
© www.shutterstock.com: 6 cr, 6 bl, 7 tr, 7cl, 7br, 8 bl, 8 br, 9 tl, 9 tr, 9 cr, 9 bl, 12 bc, 15 tl, 17 bl, 19 tl

9 br Olga Popova / Shutterstock.com, 23 tl Gary Blakeley / Shutterstock.com